Finding Birds in Sout

Introduction

'Portugal has everything that Spain has, apart from White-headed Duck, Pin-tailed Sandgrouse and ...
Duck'. So says, Peter Dedicoat, a birding guide who runs tours in both countries. Hence, although Portugal isn't as wild as parts of Andalucia and Extremadura and doesn't have many of the specialist birds in such numbers, it does offer a chance of seeing just about all the Iberian specialities including bustards, Black-shouldered Kites and Spanish Imperial Eagles. Indeed it has a few specialities of its own, especially the naturalised exotics such as Black-headed Weaver, Yellow-crowned Bishop and Crested Myna but also Ruppell's Vulture and Madeiran Storm-petrel. The petrels may be almost impossible to observe but, even so, Portugal does offer possibly the best pelagic birding in Europe, from either Fuseta or Sagres where the raptor migration invariably includes a few Ruppell's Vultures.

Portugal makes an ideal destination for anyone who wants to combine a family beach holiday with great birding. Wherever you stay in the Algarve you will be close to interesting wetland areas and also within easy reach of beautiful, wild hillsides and plains. Even the magnificent steppes between Castro Verde and Mertola are only an hour's drive from the Algarve - and they provide some of the best birding in Europe.

So, if you are travelling to the Algarve or to the equally attractive city of Lisbon, here's a guide to give you all the details you need to find the best birds within a day's drive. As ever, I've tried to make it more detailed and more helpful than any previous publications; I hope I've succeeded. To give you an even better idea of what Portugal is like from a birding point of view, there is also a DVD of the same title showing you many of the places in this book and, of course, their birds.

Have a great time in Portugal

Dave Gosney

Acknowledgements

This book is based entirely on my own observations up to 2013 but with reference to what others have reported at each site. I am particularly grateful to the locally-based birders who have been kind enough to show me around some of their favourite places and share knowledge which is passed on here, including João Ministro (proactivetur.pt), Georg Schreier (birdwatching-algarve.com), Peter Dedicoat (algarvebirders.com) and Domingos Leitao (SPEA.pt) all of whom can provide guided tours to this part of Portugal. The staff at the LPN in Entradas have also been very helpful. My visits to Portugal over the years have concentrated on sites that were recommended through correspondence with William Oliver or places I have discovered by reading other books such as 'A Birdwatchers' Guide to Portugal and Madeira' by Mooore, Elias and Costa, 'Where to Watch Birds in Spain and Portugal' by Lawrence Rose, 'Summer Birding on the Central Algarve' by Jon Hardacre and, most recently, 'Birdwatching Guide to the Algarve' by João Ministro. I've also gone in search of Portugal's exotic birds with the help of papers in Birding World and trip reports by the likes of Richard Bonser. All these sources have helped me to refine the contents of this book. However, as always, the person to whom I am most grateful is my partner Liz who continues to be such a wonderful, tolerant companion on these birdwatching expeditions and does such a fantastic job in putting together the DVDs.

The Tejo Estuary

Attraction

This area has always been good for wintering and passage waders, wildfowl and flamingoes with added attractions such as Black-shouldered Kite, Booted Eagle, Bluethroat, Collared Pratincole and flocks of Little Bustards. But in recent years it has received more attention from birders due to the presence of exotics now including not just Common Waxbills but also Black-headed Weaver, Yellow-crowned Bishop, Black-headed Munia and, nearby, Crested Myna.

Getting there

The Tejo estuary is overlooked on its western shore by Lisbon, but the best birdwatching areas are reached via the N10 in the North or the N118 to the East.

Notes

1. The area known as Lazeiras or Ponta de Erva probably offers the best birding. To get there, turn south from the N10 between Vila Franco and Porto Alto. The track (38.9329N, 8.9172W) which starts near km 113 and is marked by a large sign saying Ponta de Erva, is blocked by an automated gate. To enter, ring 969158449 and say the magic words *'Por favor, abra o portão'* (Please open the gate). This worked for us in 2013 and will work on your return provided the staff haven't gone home (check the times on the sign). Between the gate and the aerodrome the track passes through rice fields which in winter are just teeming with birds. On my last visit in January 2013 I was dazzled by vast flocks of thousands of Black-tailed Godwits plus a smattering of other assorted waders and impressive numbers of Spoonbill (at least 150) and Glossy Ibis (hundreds). If conditions are not too wet, and you've given yourself enough time, you should be able to drive on the tracks around these fields and enjoy the multitudes of birds.

2. For the next 8 kilometres you drive through uncultivated land which is great for raptors (we had Hen Harrier, Buzzard, Marsh Harrier, Peregrine and at least 5 Black-shouldered Kites). We didn't see Little Bustard but flocks of several hundred have been found here in winter. In summer this plain has breeding Montagu's Harriers and Collared Pratincoles.

3. From the building at the far end of the track (38.8344N, 8.9669W), you can overlook part of the estuary. At high tide in winter you should see hundreds of Shoveler, Teal, Wigeon, Pintail, Greylag, Dunlin, Grey Plover, Avocet and Greater Flamingo – a most impressive spectacle. You can walk right from here along an embankment which overlooks more of the estuary and areas of saltmarsh where Green Sandpiper, Waxbill, Bluethroat and Water Pipit are all easily located in winter (some French ringers had caught over 60 Bluethroats here in one winter). This path also passes drainage channels full of reedbeds which in summer have Savi's and Great Reed Warblers, Purple Herons and a few Little Bitterns. Note that you are now 12km from the entrance gate and the road is so badly potholed that you need to allow plenty of time to get back.

4. There are similar habitats on the other side of the river but access to the estuary is difficult. Drive South on the N118 from Porto Alto for 10 km then take a right turn signposted to Pancas. This road soon deteriorates into a track which, if you ignore the track to the left to Pancas, leads to a collection of farm buildings (38.8322N, 8.9131W). Turn right here, signposted 'Espadanal' but after just 200 metres you'll be confronted by a no entry sign. However, there's a car park on the left and from here you can walk for 2 km parallel to the estuary through an area of sandy fields and scattered trees that is good for raptors (harriers and Black-shouldered Kite in winter, Booted Eagle in summer), plus waxbills, waders and a chance of Little Bustard. I have walked as far as the new building (38.8489N, 8.9168W); apparently by taking the track to the right from here you can reach an area of saltpans.

5. The track which passes Pancas also overlooks the edges of the estuary and takes you through good areas for Black-shouldered Kite and Booted Eagle. However, it can be impassable by car in wet weather. It can be approached either from the 'Pancas road' to the north (turn left at 38.8283N, 8.8978W) or from the N118/IC3 in the south (38.7559N, 9.9167W).

2

Vila Franca

N10

PORTO ALTO

Rice paddies here can have thousands of godwits and hundreds of Glossy Ibis and Spoonbills

① ①

Lazeira flying club

gate can be opened electronically during work hours

② Black-shouldered Kite unmissable in winter

N118

very rough track in places

Look for Little Bustard ②

good area for BS Kite Booted Eagle, L Bustard

saltpans

② barn

No entry ④ Barrier

Turn right to 'Espadanal'

marsh

signposted to 'Pancas'

park here

salt pans or ricefields

③

vantage point Ponta de Erva

T-junction with farm buildings

walk here for Bluethroats in winter, warblers in summer

sign to Pancas estate

⑤ Booted Eagle in summer

look for hundreds of estuary birds especially Avocets

PANCAS (just a few buildings)

⑤ overlook ricefields / saltpans from this track

LAZEIRA and PANCAS

N

0   km   2

3

Alcochete

1C3

6. The ricefields to the east of Alcochete, especially around Barroca de Alva have become famous as the best area for exotics in Portugal; Alcochete itself has areas of saltpans on both sides of the town. These are treated in more detail over the page.

7. The site for Crested Myna is a few km to the east of Lisbon. From Lisbon airport you can take a ring road (Circuit 2), following signs to Estoril and Ouiera until you reach the coastal road, N6, heading west out of town. Follow this for about 13km km until you see the first of two ancient forts on the left. Continue past the first one but keep in the left hand lane so that, when you reach the next traffic lights (38.6770N, 9.3244W) you can turn left towards the second fort (sign 'Torre de Barra'). A few Crested Mynas should be easy to find on the grassy areas around the car parks here (outside either the Bar Lua de Barra or the Restaurant Torre Mar) or sometimes in the palm trees by the main road. Be circumspect about using cameras etc here; the fort itself and the office complex to the north of the main road are UN headquarters and guards may not take too kindly to you pointing lenses in their direction.

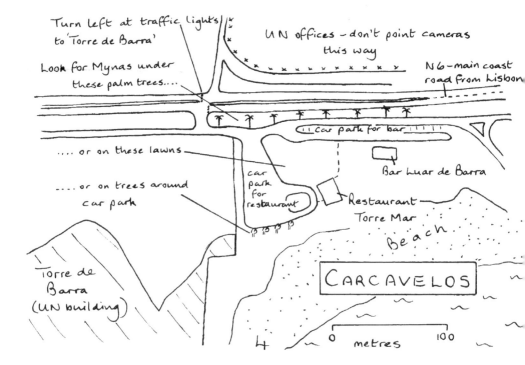

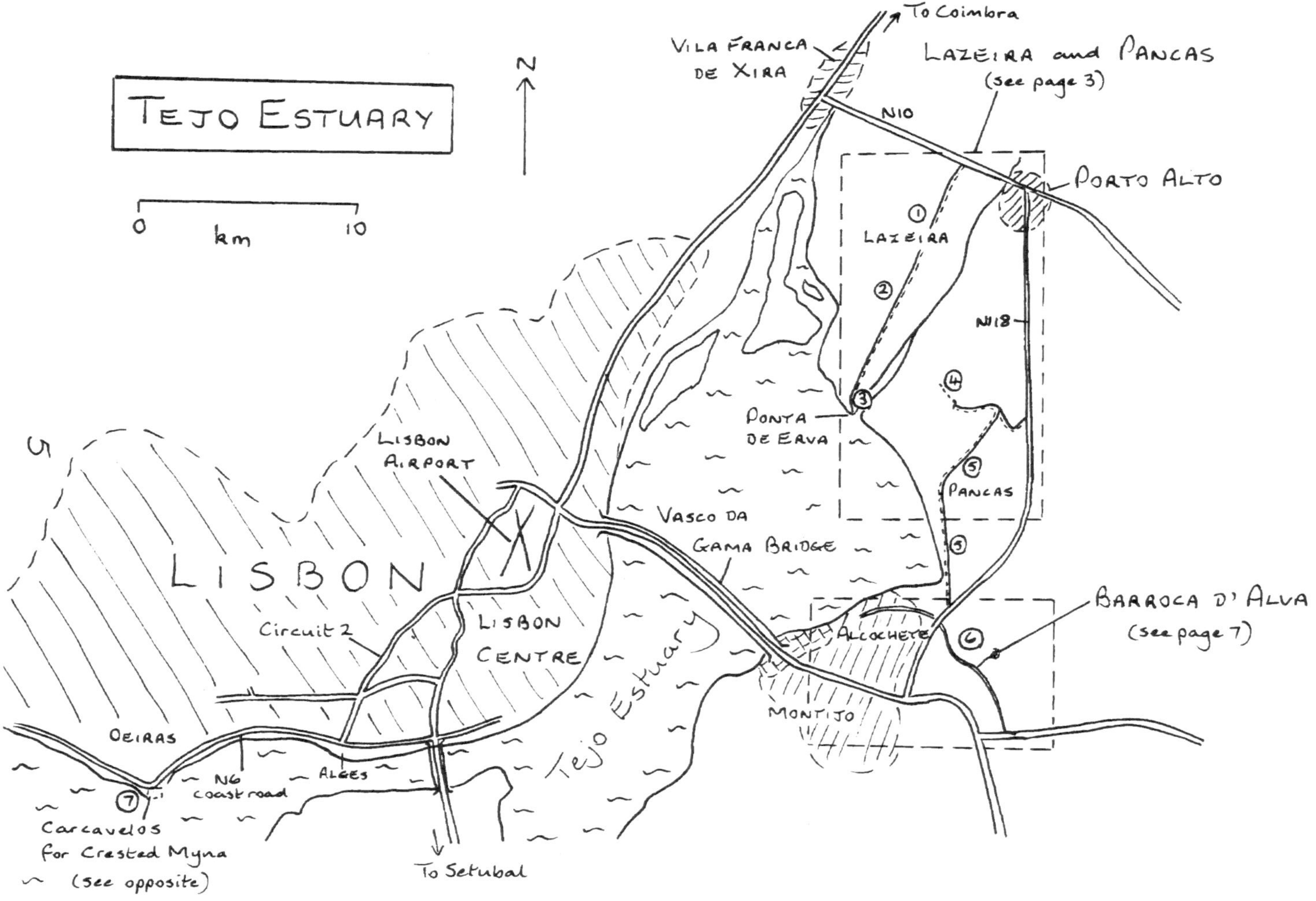

TEJO ESTUARY

N ←

km
0   10

To Coimbra

LAZEIRA and PANCAS (see page 3)

PORTO ALTO

BARROCA D'ALVA (See page 7)

VILA FRANCA DE XIRA

N10

LAZEIRA

②
①

N118

④

PANCAS

⑤

PONTA DE ERVA

③

⑥

⑦ (near Alcochete)

ALCOCHETE

MONTIJO

VASCO DA GAMA BRIDGE

Tejo Estuary

LISBON

LISBON AIRPORT

LISBON CENTRE

Circuit 2

ALGÉS

N6 coast road

To Setubal

OEIRAS

CARCAVELOS
For Crested Myna
(see opposite)

⑦

5

Barroca d'Alva

Attraction

This area has come to birders' attention as a site for some of Portugal's naturalised exotic species, notably Black-headed Weaver, Yellow-crowned Bishop and Black-headed Munia as well as the more widespread Common Waxbill. The area also has extensive marshes, saltpans and views over the Tagus estuary.

Getting there

From Lisbon, take the A12 (=IP1) across the new Vasco da Gama bridge then, after crossing the estuary, turn north on the IC3 towards Alcochete. The next major turn off, after about 3km, leads to a roundabout (38.7453N, 8.9300W). From there you can turn left (north-west) to Alcochete or right, signposted to Pegões, towards the birding sites at Barroca d'Alva and Rilvas.

Notes

1. About 3km along the Pegões road you reach a roundabout with a left turn signposted to Barroca. Take this road and park close to the bridge at 38.7280 N 8.9050 W. This is the spot that was recommended in Birding World (Vol 21 page 203). The reeds on either side of the bridge often have groups of Common Waxbill, smaller numbers of Black-headed Weaver and a few Yellow-crowned Bishop, especially at dusk when all these species come to roost here. This same patch of reeds also has Reed Warblers and the occasional Little Bittern.

2. 600 metres further along the same road is a drainage channel on the right, edged with tall reeds in which it may be easier to see the exotics during the day. There were obviously birds in the saltpans and marshes to the west of this road but they were rarely visible except when they took off. As well as the expected Mallard, Shoveler and Marsh Harrier, I've had flocks of Spoonbills and Glossy Ibis and a Ruddy Shelduck.

3. Another site for the exotics is found beyond Barroca. Go through the village and keep left along a track to the north. Park at 38.7411N, 8.8923W and walk east along a track with reeds on your left and fields on your right. The three species of exotics regularly flit between the reeds and the fields.

4. If you return to the Pegões road and turn left (south) at the roundabout, you reach the N4 after another 2 km. Turn left here and look for tracks to the right after the O Paul restaurant. The first of these leads to a farmhouse, opposite which are some trees and bushes (38.7015N 8.8766W) where David Monticelli found 4 Black-headed Munias (Birding World), though I failed to find them on my visits in 2008 and 2012 . I also tried another site, along the next track which leads to the hamlet of Rilvas, and failed there too. Many other birders have struggled to find this species which may now be easier at Zambujal (site 2, page 8).

5. On the east side of Alcochete is a reserve with a visitor centre, observation point and a walk to an area of old saltpans. From the IC3, follow signs to Alcochete until, 2 km beyond the first roundabout, look for a minor road that cuts back to the right, signposted to Sitia das Hortas. This area is good for estuarine species including Black-tailed Godwit and Avocet.

6. A much better area of saltpans is found to the west of Alcochete where impressive flocks of estuarine waders roost at high tide. Encouragingly this area is designated as a nature reserve with a nature trail and viewing facilities including hides. Frustratingly though, it is CLOSED TO THE PUBLIC except on Fridays when guided walks are available (email: contacto@salinasdosamouco.pt). At other times you can see only a fraction of the area; the best bet is to take the track nearest to Alcochete, signposted 'Salines do Samouco'. Although this leads to gates with no entry signs, it passes saltpans that can have hundreds of birds such as Kentish Plover and also gives access to a car park overlooking the estuary.

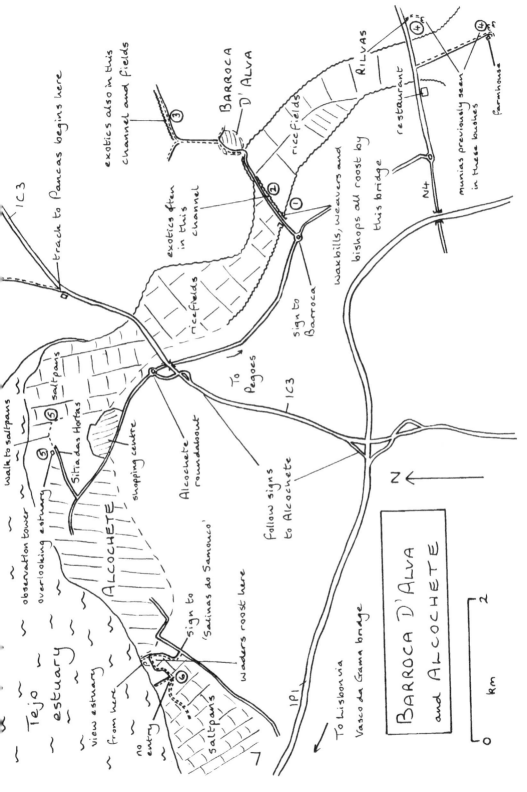

BARROCA D'ALVA and ALCOCHETE

Tejo estuary

walk to saltpans
observation tower overlooking estuary
view estuary from here
saltpans
Sitia das Hortas
shopping centre
ALCOCHETE
Alcochete roundabout
Follow signs to Alcochete
sign to 'Salinas do Samouco'
waders roost here
no entry
saltpans

⑤
⑤

To Pegoes
IC3

IC3
track to Pancas begins here
exotics also in this channel and fields
③
exotics often in this channel

BARROCA D'ALVA

ricefields
ricefields
②
①
sign to Barroca
Waxbills, weavers and bishops all roost by this bridge
RILVAS
restaurant
N4

⑦

④

munias previously seen in these bushes
farmhouse

N

To Lisbon via Vasco da Gama bridge
IP1

⑥

0   km   2

The Sado Estuary

Attraction

This is an excellent estuary which, at least in winter and during passage times, offers several places where you should see lots of birds. Inevitably waders are the main attraction with hundreds, if not thousands of Avocet, Black-tailed Godwit, Grey Plover, Dunlin, Redshank etc., but I've also had flamingoes, ibis, mergansers, grebes, egrets and raptors including Peregrine, Hen Harrier and Black-shouldered Kite. The rice fields here also support a range of exotics including Yellow-crowned Bishop and, reportedly, 2 species of munia.

Getting there

The Sado Estuary is a large bay with Setubal at its north-west corner. It is encircled by over 100km of main roads (don't underestimate the distances involved) but you need to find smaller roads to get access to the best areas.

Notes

1. Starting from Setubal, drive about 10 km east on the N10 and look for a right turn to 'Gambia' with signs for a campsite. Follow this to a T-junction, turn right and then keep left for 3 km until an area of old saltpans can be seen on the left. There are signs indicating that this is now a nature reserve and there are observation towers too but I could find no way of reaching these. Entrance is clearly forbidden at the main gate to the saltpans (38.5431N, 8.7627W) but there's a second gate to the left through which you can at least reach the edge of the pans. However, in two visits I've seen little here – the pans seem to be rather old and overgrown and generally too deep to be productive, though maybe there are better spots out of view. Further views of the estuary can be had by following the track (now sandy) for two more kilometres to the end of the wood, where I've heard Great Spotted Cuckoo.

2. Returning to the main road, continue for another 2 km until, after the railway station ('Aguas de Moura') and immediately after the big white buildings for storing rice, you see a road to the right (38.5768N, 8.7441W) signposted 'reserva natural' (coming from the opposite direction, you only see the back of this sign). This leads to a bridge over the river to Zambujal which you can now only cross on foot. Both Black-headed and Scaly-breasted Munias have been seen from the tracks around the saltpans but I have only had Waxbills, both here and in the overgrown fields and gardens across the bridge. Scan for estuarine birds from the bridge, including hundreds of Avocets and Black-tailed Godwits and, in winter, parties of mergansers. Don't forget to walk back along the road to check the rice fields on either side – in 2012 I had 2 singing Yellow-crowned Bishops to the west of the road (38.5730N, 8.7397W).

3. The east side of the estuary is said to have 3 main attractions: views of roosting waders from the shore at Pineiro, an attractive wetland at Lagoa de Bem Pais (for Marsh Harrier, herons and wintering Penduline Tit) and extensive wader-filled saltpans at Monte Novo. However, in 2 visits I've been unable to find Pineiro and Bem Pais; I've put a map online to show where (not?) to drive in search of them (www.easybirder.co.uk/extramaps). The saltpans at Monte Novo have now been converted entirely to rice fields but can still be full of birds; in October 2012 there were hundreds of egrets and storks and over 100 Glossy Ibis. Monte Novo is signposted from the N5; the ricefields can be viewed from the edge of the village (38.4300N, 8.6362W).

4. The Lagoa de Murta, about 19 km from the junction at Alcocer do Sal, is probably the best of several small wetlands on the south side of the estuary. It is easily missed but, by parking near km 7.6 (38.4054N, 8.7122W), you can find a small track to the south around the left side of a dense patch of willows. [There's a sign on the next track saying 'sanctuario, no entry' but I think that is merely to deter people from driving up that track into the wood.] The willows can be good for small birds; I've had Penduline Tit, Waxbill, 'Iberian' Chiff-chaff, Green Woodpecker, Crested Tit and lots of Cetti's Warblers. The lake itself has proved relatively dull, with waterbirds such as Mallard, Teal, Little Grebe and Grey Heron but at the right time of day or year you should also see roosting or breeding herons which have included both Great Bittern and Night Heron.

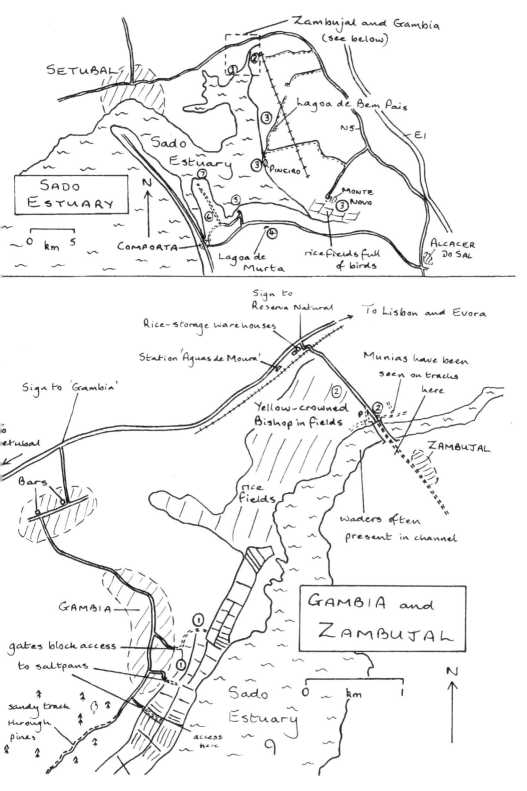

Sado Estuary map (top):

SETUBAL

Zambujal and Gambia
(see below)

Sado Estuary

Lagoa de Bem Pais

N5

E1

① ②

③

③ PINEIRO

⑦

⑤

⑥

④

MONTE NOVO ③

SADO ESTUARY

N

0 km 5

COMPORTA

Lagoa de Murta

ricefields full of birds

ALCACER DO SAL

Gambia and Zambujal map (bottom):

Sign to Reserva Natural

Rice-storage warehouses

Station 'Aguas de Moura'

To Lisbon and Evora

Munias have been seen on tracks here

Sign to 'Gambia'

To Setubal

Yellow-crowned Bishop in fields

② ②

ZAMBUJAL

Bars

rice fields

waders often present in channel

GAMBIA

GAMBIA and ZAMBUJAL

gates block access to saltpans

①

①

Sado Estuary

sandy track through pines

access here

0 km 1

N

9

5. The best estuarine area I've found is near Carrusqueira, about 3 km beyond Lake Murta. Keep right in the village and follow the best road you can until you reach the edge of the estuary (38.4128N, 8.7561W); walk and view from there. At high tide in winter I've had thousands of roosting waders nearby including several hundred each of Ringed Plover, Dunlin, Redshank, Grey Plover and Curlew. There were also over 100 each of Shoveler, Avocet and Greater Flamingo and smaller numbers of Wigeon, Pintail, Red-breasted Merganser, Cormorant and Whimbrel. Other birds included Peregrine, Black-necked Grebe, Water Pipit, Fan-tailed Warbler and Waxbill.

6. Nearby is an extensive area of ricefields which, as ever, attract hundreds of herons, egrets and Glossy Ibis. In October 2012 I also had flocks of over 100 flava wagtails and over 50 Northern Wheatears. The area is good for raptors too, especially towards dusk when Hen Harriers come to roost and Black-shouldered Kites are hunting (I had at least 4). To reach this area, look for a left turn in Carrusqueira, signposted to Aldea do Possanco. Follow this road for 3 km to a T-junction then turn right on a road that turns into a track. After 750 metres, immediately before the first big drainage channel, turn right (38.4014N, 8.7802W) and follow this track through 5 km of rice fields.

7. At the end of this track is a T-junction immediately before the dyke which defends the paddies from the estuary. You can drive left or right from here to explore a series of pools (eg 38.4412N, 8.7995W) inside the dyke (good for waders, flava wagtails and, reportedly, rails) or you can climb the dyke at several points to look out across the estuary for the usual estuary birds including Black-necked Grebe and mergansers in winter.

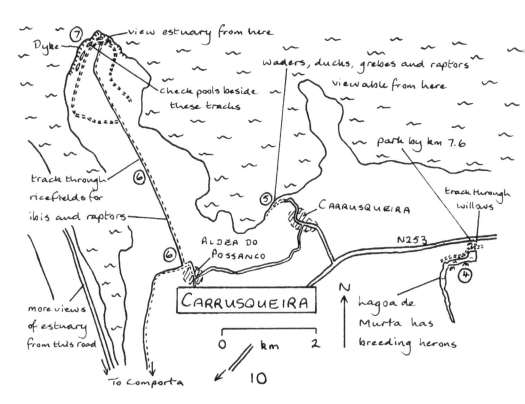

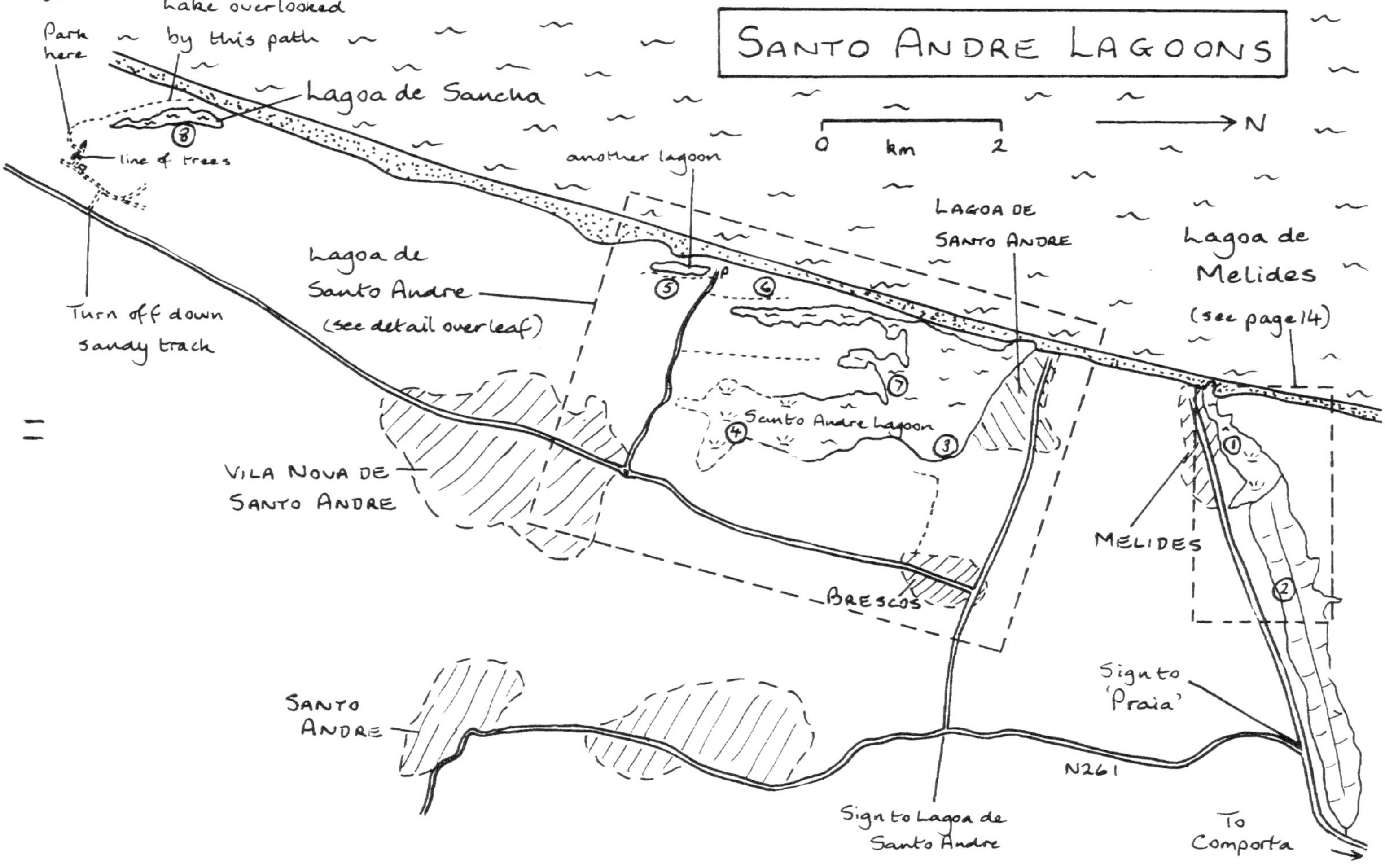

SANTO ANDRE LAGOONS

N

Lagoa de Melides

(see page 14)

MELIDES

Signto 'Praia'

N261

To Comporta

Sign to Lagoa de Santo Andre

SANTO ANDRE

BRESCOS

LAGOA DE SANTO ANDRE

Lagoa de Santo Andre
(see detail overleaf)

Santo Andre Lagoon

VILA NOVA DE SANTO ANDRE

0   km   2

Lagoa de Sancha

lake overlooked by this path

another lagoon

Park here

line of trees

Turn off down sandy track

11

Santo Andre Lagoons

Attraction

These three coastal lagoons, north of Sines, together hold several interesting species such as Little Bittern, Purple Heron, Great Reed Warbler, Savi's Warbler and, in winter, Red-crested Pochard, Glossy Ibis, Spoonbill, Bluethroat and rafts of ducks. However, the best areas require some walking and others are either inaccessible or difficult to find.

Getting there

From Sines take the N261-3 towards Lisbon then turn left on the N261 towards Melides. The three lagoons are on roads to the left, Sancha via an obscure track and the others via roads to 'Lagoa de Santo Andre' and 'Praia de Melides'.

Notes

1. The road to the beach (Praia) from Melides passes the Lagoa de Melides on the right. The lagoon can be reached by taking the next track to the right (38.1315N, 8.7780W) after the Leito de Bairrada café. Where this track ends you can overlook both the lagoon (gulls, ducks, coot) and a sizeable reedbed that has at least Marsh Harriers, Cetti's Warblers and waxbills.

2. You might find there are actually more birds in the ricefields just upstream. You can park by a set of gates labelled Monte dos Pousatais and walk the track through the gates (38.1327N, 8.7715W) to the ricefields. If water levels are suitable you should see lots of storks and herons; I also had over 100 Glossy Ibis. From the track I also had a party of Azure-winged Magpies and a singing Woodlark.

3. The easiest vantage point for the Lagoa de Santo Andre is found by taking the beach road towards the Lagoa de Santo Andre resort but, before you reach the village, turn left on a sandy track (38.1101N, 8.7776W) signposted to a 'Centro do Campo' (Field Centre). You can view the lake from near this centre or get closer by taking the track to the west and, before you reach the campsite, walking left towards the shore (38.1055N, 8.7841W). The tracks around here are good for passerines: I had Iberian Grey Shrike, Woodlark, Nuthatch, Short-toed Treecreeper, Cirl Bunting, Cetti's Warbler and Pied and Spotted Flycatchers. In winter, the water is covered with birds but these are mostly Coot. However you should also spot a range of ducks, cormorants, stilts, flamingoes and herons including Spoonbills and Great White Egrets (I had 2 in September 2012). The same bay and more of the lake can also be seen by taking the track immediately after the bridge just South of Brescos village, an area which looks generally good for small birds (I've had Waxbills here).

4. Probably the best bet for the key reedbed species at Santo Andre (Purple Heron, Little Bittern, Great Reed Warbler, Savi's Warbler and wintering Bluethroat and Penduline Tit) is the reedbed at the southern end of the lake. I tried to reach here using directions given in Moore *et al* but the only likely-looking track ended in a fenced off area (38.0836N, 8.7779W) with signs saying 'Observatorio de Aves: entrada prohibida' – along with pictures of birds in the hand. Not exactly visitor-friendly.

5. There is however another promising reedbed at Lagoa de Monte Velho (also known as Lagoa de Vacaria). To get there, continue south down the east side of the main lake and turn right at the next roundabout signposted 'Praia do Monte Velho'. The car park (38.0808N, 8.8088W) at the end of this road overlooks the pool which is entirely reed-covered. A walk past this pool in late September produced only Waxbills but in spring there could be Little Bittern and Purple Heron.

6. Returning on the same road it may be worth stopping at the next car park (38.0792N, 8.80792W) and walking north through coastal heath for 800 metres to an observatorio (38.0864N, 8.8051W) which is open to the public. It's nothing more than a screen with viewing holes but it does get you close to the south end of one arm of the lake. In September 2012 there were few birds here, just a scattering of ducks and herons but it may be better at other times.

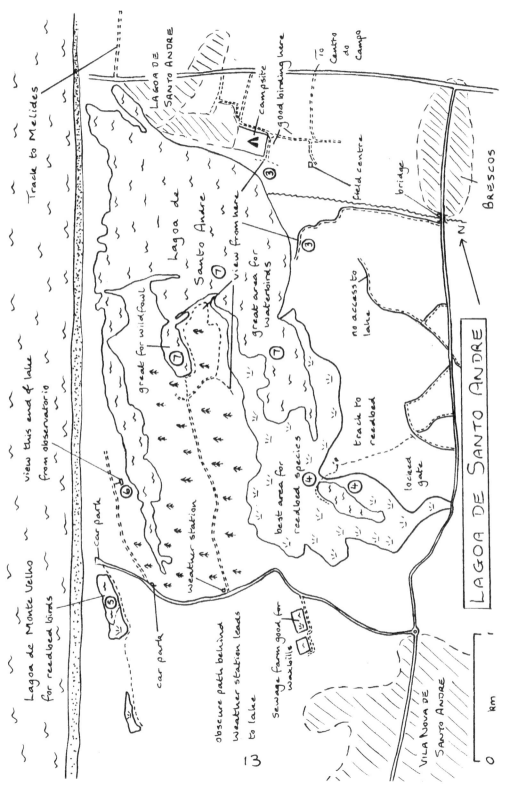

Lagoa de Monte Velho for reedbed birds

Track to Melides

view this end of lake from observatorio

LAGOA DE SANTO ANDRE

Lagoa de Santo Andre

To Centro do Campo

campsite

good birding here

③

field centre

bridge

Brescos

N

Lagoa de Santo Andre

view from here

⑦

great for wildfowl

⑦

great area for waterbirds

⑦

no access to lake

track to reedbed

best area for reedbed species

④

④

locked gate

car park

obscure path behind weather station leads to lake

weather station

car park

⑥

⑤

Sewage Farm good for waxbills

Vila Nova de Santo Andre

LAGOA DE SANTO ANDRE

0   km

13

7. The best part of the lake is reached via another path, 800 metres further inland. Park by a gate (38.0765N, 8.7984W) to a little white building (weather station?) and walk north, via a gap in the fence for pedestrians. A local map suggests there should be two more observatorios along this path but I couldn't find any. Apart from a few migrants such as redstarts and flycatchers, and resident birds such as Crested Tits, the pine plantation is likely to be rather dull until the path reaches a T-junction and pools come into view. From this point there are two pools ahead of you which can be teeming with wildfowl (Shoveler, Gadwall, Teal, Mallard) or you can follow the track to the right until you reach the main part of the lake. From here you can see many of the birds you saw from site 3 but the birds will be closer to this undisturbed shoreline. As well as flamingoes, spoonbills and Great White Egrets I also had Marsh Harrier, 2 Hobbies and an Osprey.

8. The Lagoa de Sancha is said to be good for reed-bed birds including Little Bittern and wintering Bluethroats but is almost impossible to find. There are details of how to get there, with a map, at www.easybirder.co.uk/extramaps but I should add that when I visited here in September 2012 it was practically devoid of birds. Indeed it looked as though the reedbed was dying from the centre outwards due to some form of pollution, though there was still enough of a reedbed left to support the key species.

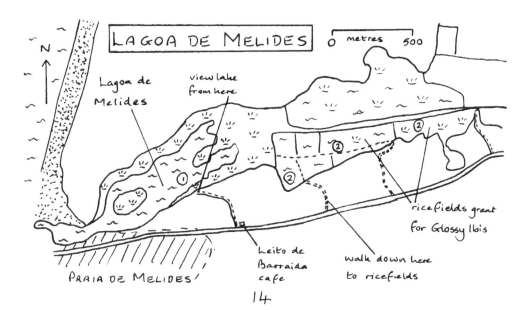

14

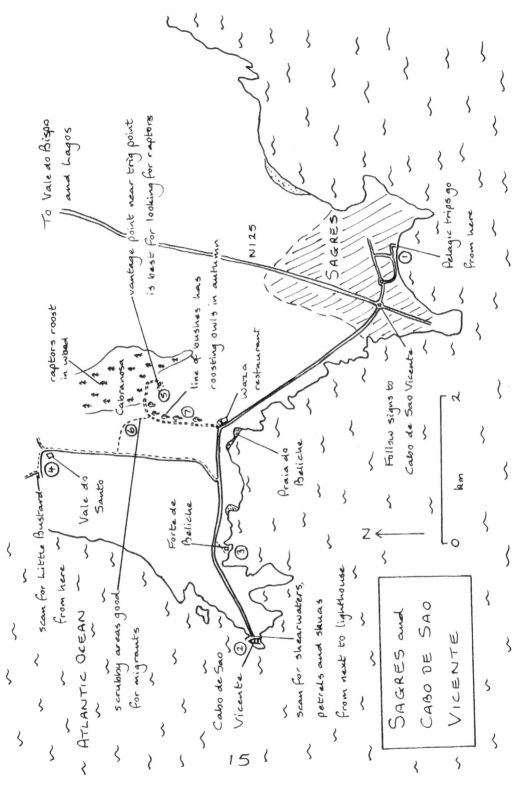

SAGRES and CABO DE SAO VICENTE

To Vale ao Bispo and Lagos

vantage point near trig point is best for looking for raptors

raptors roost in wood

line of bushes has roosting owls in autumn

Cabranosa

⑤

⑦

⑥

Waza restaurant

N125

SAGRES

Pelagic trips go from here

①

Follow signs to Cabo de Sao Vicente

ATLANTIC OCEAN

scan for Little Bustard from here

Vale do Santo

④

scrubby areas good for migrants

Forte de Beliche

③

Praia do Beliche

N ←

0   km   2

Cabo de Sao Vicente

②

scan for shearwaters, petrels and skuas from next to lighthouse

15

The Sagres peninsula

Attraction

Since this is the south-west corner of Europe, it has obvious potential as a watchpoint for migrants. Raptors have been well-studied with up to 17 species a day in the autumn but this is also a great place for observing migrant passerines, seabirds and even owls. The seabirds, including regular Balearic and Great Shearwaters and Wilson's Petrels, are best seen by taking pelagic trips which are easily available from Sagres.

Getting there

Follow the N125 west of Lagos to Sagres. As you approach Sagres, Cabo de São Vicente is signposted to the right at the first junction.

Notes

1. There are two companies in the harbour (Baleeira) of Sagres which offer pelagic trips for birdwatchers. For example marilimitado.com charge 40 Euros for a morning session (3-4 hours) on a Rigid Inflatable Boat which includes going a couple of miles off Cabo São Vicente and chumming where the continental shelf drops away or going further out to wherever the fishing fleet is pulling in flocks of birds. Avoid going on a Sunday or National holiday, as there will be no fishing boats, or Monday when the chum will be more than a day old and not so 'magnetic'. Trips are available daily until October, after which the weather may occasionally prevent a sailing. Throughout June to November, Cory's and Balearic Shearwaters are guaranteed and the crew will take you close to any rafts that are on the sea. Except when there are no fishing boats you should also see species such as Manx, Sooty and Great Shearwater (the latter is most numerous in October and November), Storm and Wilson's Petrel (the latter peaks in August and may be gone by October), possibly all 4 species of skua, (with Great Skua the most numerous and Long-tailed the scarcest) and there's a chance of Grey Phalarope, Little Shearwater, Leach's Petrel and Sabine's Gull too.

2. Of course, there's a chance of seeing all these birds from the headland of Cabo de São Vicente but the vantage point is very high so even birds close to shore look rather small. Nearby rocky islets are used by breeding Yellow-legged Gulls and Choughs. The Cape is a flat, featureless plateau covered in bushes which are invariably less than knee-high so not so productive for passerine migrants.

3. Just inland from the Cape, the obvious Forte de Beliche is a site for wintering Alpine Accentor.

4. A little further inland, 2.2 km from the lighthouse, a sandy track (37.0275N, 8.9715W) leads north (marked by a metal post covered in stickers). Drive 2 km along this track and stop near the farm building (Vale do Santo). The open areas visible from here are often good for Little Bustard and sometimes passage Dotterel too. If you fail here, continue north along this track and keep scanning.

5. Migrating raptors seem to congregate around the wood at Cabranosa. To reach the best viewing point, take the sandy track (37.0273N, 8.9630W) immediately west of the Waza restaurant and follow it along the western edge of a line of bushes., Turn right when you reach the wood, then fork left on a sandy track towards a trig point (37.0356N, 8.9541W). In autumn, at least, the route may be signposted to Cabranosa and you should see other birders scanning from the hillock next to the trig point. Each autumn about 5000 raptors are counted here. At the time of the Sagres birdwatching festival (early October) the most impressive are the flocks of Booted Eagles and Griffon Vulture (often over 100 of each per day) but Short-toed Eagle, Red Kite, Black Kite, Sparrowhawk, Peregrine, Hobby and Hen Harrier are seen daily too. At other times Honey Buzzards, Montagu's Harriers and White Storks are more numerous. Perhaps surprisingly, rarer species such as Pallid Harrier, Spanish Imperial Eagle, Long-legged Buzzard and Eleonora's Falcon are seen in most years and you should check every bird in any vulture flocks as up to 3 Ruppell's Vultures may linger for several days.

6. The woodland and scrub near here also provides the best cover for migrant passerines. In early October we had a suite of flycatchers, redstarts, whinchats, whitethroats etc plus a Bonelli's Warbler, a Wryneck and a Grasshopper Warbler caught at the ringing station where ringing demonstations are given to the public during the Sagres brding festival. At least in the autumn, this is also the best area to look for the local Red-billed Choughs which circle around the wood in a flock of about 80 birds.

7. The line of bushes between the wood and the main road has roosting owls in the autumn. They are almost impossible to find during the day but, somewhat improbably, they can be observed at dusk leaving the bushes and flying high as if setting off on the next leg of their migration. Up to a dozen Long-eared/Short-eared Owls can be counted by standing at the far end of the bushes (37.0372N, 8.9588W) and scanning to the west at dusk.

8. The best wetland close to Sagres is the Lagoa de Budens but it is almost completely overgrown by a reedbed so relatively few waterbirds are seen here. However, a walk along its southern edge takes you through lovely lush habitat which, in the autumn, is often full of migrants, especially warblers, flycatchers and redstarts. In spring the songbirds include Savi's Warbler, Great Reed Warbler and Iberian Chiffchaff and Water Rails call from the reeds. Look out for waxbills, Azure-winged Magpies, Purple Herons and Marsh Harriers here too. To get there turn south from the N125 near the Intermarche store, signposted to Budens. After 2 km, turn left signposted to Burgau and follow this road until you see the marsh on your left (37.0729N, 8.8061W).

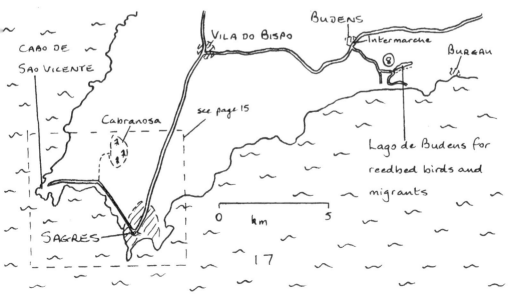

The Alvor Estuary

Attraction

In the 1990's this was probably the best-watched birding site in Portugal thanks to the enthusiasm of the staff and visitors to the Cruzinha bird observatory. Rarities in 1993 alone included Paddyfield Warbler, Royal Tern, Lesser Yellowlegs, Pectoral Sandpiper and Yellow-browed Warbler giving some idea of the potential, not just of this site, but of sites throughout the Algarve. More recently, the observatory has concentrated its efforts on other taxa; hence, although there is still a ringing station, fewer rarities are now being found. Even so, the estuary is another good site for species such as Caspian Tern, Audouin's Gull, Greater Flamingo, Bluethroat and Water Pipit. Black-shouldered Kite is now a regular visitor too.

Getting there

Follow the main road (N125) west from Portimao and look out, after about 9 km, for a signposted right turn to Mexiloheira Grande. Exactly opposite this road is an unlikely-looking track to the left, down the side of a garden centre with potted palm trees; this is the track to the Quinta da Rocha, a headland between two estuaries. The track passes the observatory at Cruzinha and continues to the 'western marsh'.

Notes

1. The ringing station itself is run by a Christian charity, A Rocha. It is open to visitors on Thursdays only (10 - 12.30), when the staff and volunteers will be happy to show you birds in the hand, answer your questions about local birds and sell you their publications including a bird report. Most of the birds are caught in their garden, an area typical of the rest of Quinta da Rocha, with highlights such as Hoopoe, Little Owl, Sardinian Warbler and, sometimes waxbills. Apparently 3 pairs of Red-necked Nightjars breed in the area. There is a small car park near the entrance (37.1439N, 8.6077W)

2. The rough grassy area just east of the fishtanks is the best bet for waxbills.

3. By parking where the track ends (37.1341N, 8.6131W), you can then walk across the 'western marsh' to the old salinas. This is a very good area; Caspian Terns can be seen in winter in the saltpans and Water Pipit, Kingfisher and waders on the marsh.

4. The open estuary is easiest to view from the sea wall. The sandspits are roosting areas for huge numbers of gulls and a few terns, especially Sandwich and Caspian. Audouin's Gulls occur regularly amongst the gulls, especially in winter when Peregrines hunt over the estuary.

5. The area of bushes at the tip of the headland looks great for migrants; there were plenty of Redwings and Song Thrushes in February.

6. The estuary can also be viewed, in better light, from the promontory across the south of the bay. To get there, follow signs to Alvor from the N125, continue through Monte de Alvor and keep going, following signs to 'Praia'. There are several boardwalks across the dunes but the one furthest inland offers the best views of the estuary. This begins (37.1257N, 8.5975W) behind the football pitches of the 'complexo desportivo' (sports centre).

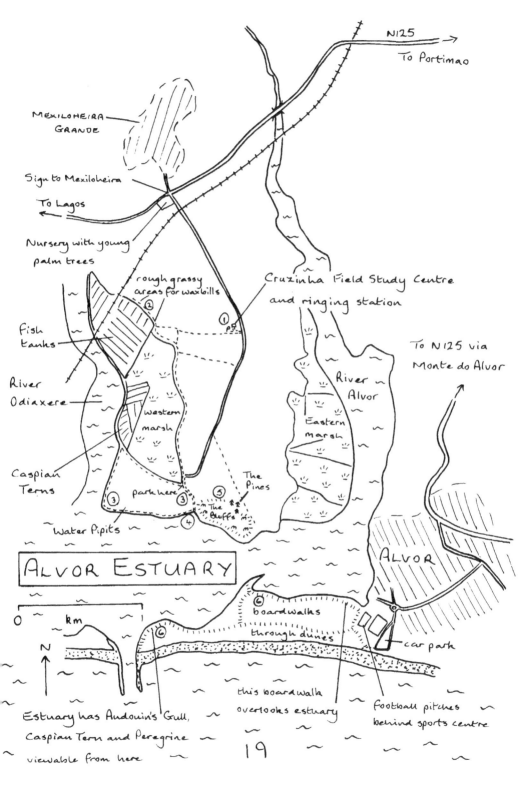

N125
To Portimao

MEXILOHEIRA GRANDE

Sign to Mexiloheira

To Lagos

Nursery with young palm trees

rough grassy areas for waxbills

② ①

Cruzinha Field Study Centre and ringing station

Fish tanks

River Odiaxere

Western marsh

River Alvor

Eastern marsh

To N125 via Monte do Alvor

Caspian Terns

park here

③ ③

⑤ The Pines

④ The Bluffs

Water Pipits

ALVOR ESTUARY

0   km   1

N

ⓒ

ⓒ

ⓒ boardwalks through dunes

ALVOR

car park

this boardwalk overlooks estuary

football pitches behind sports centre

Estuary has Audouin's Gull, Caspian Tern and Peregrine viewable from here

19

Lagoa de Salgado (Pêra Marsh)

Attraction

Probably the best wetland along the Algarve coast. If water levels are good it can be teeming with a variety of ducks, waders, herons and other waterbirds including breeding Purple Gallinule, all of which can be watched at relatively close range. Owners of the nearby golf course have in the past been guilty of draining the site completely to avoid flooding their greens but there is now an agreement that this will not be repeated so the site should get better as it becomes a more permanent wetland.

Getting there

From the A22, either take the turning to (junction 8) and follow signs to Praia Grande or, to avoid getting lost in the small streets of Pêra, take the turning to Armação de Pêra (junction 7) and keep following signs to there until you see a camp site (campismo) on your right. Turn left at the next roundabout (signposted Albufeira) and, at the second roundabout on this road (37.1095N, 8.3345W), turn sharp right signposted to Praia Grande. Follow this road until you see the lake on your left.

Notes

1. The car park (37.0972N, 8.3341W) at the northern end of the lagoon can be a fantastic place to stand and scan for ducks, herons and waders, especially in the afternoon with the light behind you. In October 2012 the flocks of birds included Ruff, Spotted Redshank, Avocet, Little Stint, Black-tailed Godwit, Lapwing, Audouin's Gull, Spoonbill, Flamingo and Glossy Ibis. The 4 Bald Ibis that were here in 2009 (captive bred birds from a failed re-introduction scheme in Spain) have now disappeared.

2. From the car park (37.0957N, 8.3365W) nearest the beach, there is a boardwalk path between the lagoon and the seaward dunes. You can get more views of the lagoon from here, including areas near the beach which can't be seen from site 1. This is the most likely area where Purple Swamphens can be seen well, especially on the reedy bank close to the golfcourse, where Squacco Herons are regularly seen and Black-headed Weavers and their nests can be spotted. It is also the best area for diving duck such as Pochard which should be checked for Ferruginous Duck as they have bred here at least twice. The reeds and bushes close to the water are likely to have Reed, Sardinian and Fan-tailed Warblers and this is a great place to look for Little Bittern. Short-toed Larks breed in the dunes, where I have also seen Collared Pratincole. From the beach I've had very close views of Cory's Shearwaters in autumn and Great Skuas in spring.

3. It's also worth walking from the beach car park in the opposite direction to check the scattered bushes for migrants. In October 2012 there were loads of Whinchats and Wheatears and other species such as Subalpine Warbler, Woodchat Shrike and 2 Short-eared Owls. In spring, Red-necked Nightjars call at dusk from near the ruined building.

4. There's another wetland just 1.5 km to the west which can attract many of the species at the main lagoon although the water level is unreliable. Before you reach the main lake, turn right, following signs to Carlos's Beach Bar where there is room for several cars. Park here (37.0992N, 8.3472W) and walk towards Armação de Pêra aiming for a spot beyond the clump of pine bushes. From there you can scan the marsh for birds such as Purple Heron or walk alongside a wall to get closer to the pools if they are there. In spring you should see Short-toed Larks in the dunes. In 2013 this area couldn't be viewed from the Armação de Pêra side due to building works.

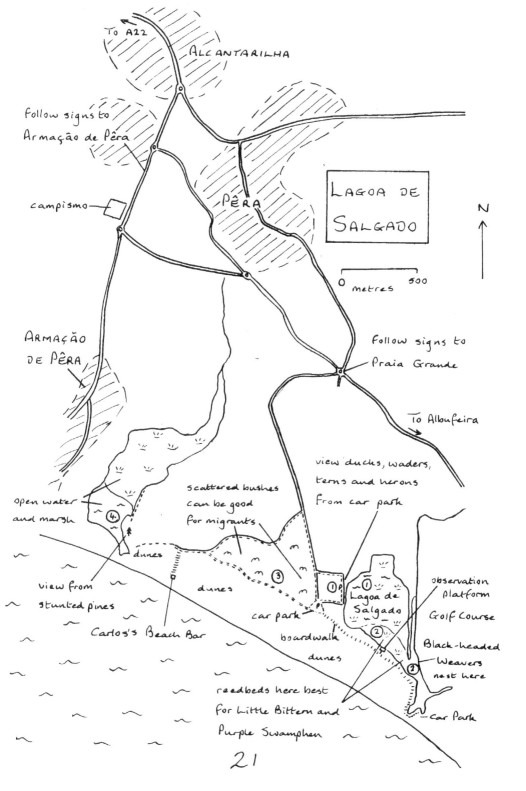

To A22

ALCANTARILHA

Follow signs to
Armação de Pêra

campismo

PÊRA

LAGOA DE
SALGADO

N

0 metres 500

ARMAÇÃO
DE PÊRA

Follow signs to
Praia Grande

To Albufeira

view ducks, waders,
terns and herons
from car park

scattered bushes
can be good
for migrants

open water
and marsh

④

③

dunes

view from
stunted pines

dunes

② Lagoa de
Salgado

observation
platform

Golf Course

Carlos's Beach Bar

① ①

①

car park

boardwalk

②

Black-headed
Weavers
nest here

dunes

②

reedbeds here best
for Little Bittern and
Purple Swamphen

car park

21

Vilamoura – Falesia lagoon and the Parque Ambiental

Attraction

Vilamoura is a new town built especially for tourists whose idea of paradise is very different from mine but it is blessed with two reasonable birding spots within walking distance – a lake (Falesia lagoon) and mixed habitats, including reedbeds, in the Parque Ambiental. In addition to the usual ducks, herons and reedbed warblers, the area has Purple Gallinule, Little Bittern and Black-headed Weaver.

Getting there

To get to Vilamoura from the A22, take the Boliqueime turning (junction 11) then turn left along the N125 towards Faro for 3 km until you see a right turn to Vilamoura. The two birding sites can be reached by turning west from this road into town.

Notes

1. Coming from the R125, turn right at the third roundabout (37.1025N, 8.1243W). Follow this road (the Avda de Albufeira) for about 2.5 km past 4 more roundabouts then turn left (south) at the next roundabout (37.1111N, 8.1489W), ignoring the 'no through road' sign. Meander through a car park and follow the best lane you can, as far as a big gate (37.1073N, 8.1510W) on the right, signposted Vilamoura Parque Ambiental.

2. The path through the gates takes you around the back of a sports field. Listen for Golden Orioles in the copse to your right and look for Woodchat Shrikes and Bee-eaters on the wires to the left.

3. By walking to the far end of the sports field you reach a field with a marshy pool in it. The track around the right-hand side of this field gives access to a hide (37.0966N, 8.1494W) overlooking the pool. On my visit this just had birds such as Little Grebe and Moorhen but the walk around the lane produced Melodious Warbler, Cetti's Warbler, Quail and Serin. Birds such as Purple Gallinule, Marsh Harrier and Purple Heron have been seen at this pool.

4. There is another hide (37.0916N, 8.1426W) which is more productive but faces south-east so the light is poor from here except in late afternoon. This is a delightful spot, though there are usually only a few grebes and ducks on the open water. It is the reedbed that provides the most interest as this is one of the best places in Portugal to get really close to Purple Swamphen and, in spring, you should at least hear both Little Bittern and Great Reed Warbler. Some of the reeds are very close to the hide so if a Little Bittern does pop up it should give excellent views. Grey Herons seem to have a heronry at the far end of the pool and Purple Herons and Marsh Harriers often fly by. Black-headed Weavers can be spotted in the reeds and there must be a good chance of getting crakes here on passage.

5. Site 4 can be reached via shorter route taking in more good birding spots: follow the main road into Vilamoura until it becomes a dual carriageway; turn right at the next junction (37.0926N, 8.1275W) and continue for 750 metres before taking the next left (37.0931N, 8.1346W). You can drive this dusty track until you see another track to the left with a sign saying 'no access for vehicles'. Park here (37.0957N, 8.1405W) and walk that track for 450 metres until you see a sign to the observatorio. Along the walk, check the bushes over the channel on your right for Night Heron, Common Waxbill and breeding Black-headed Weavers. The sewage ponds on your right can be viewed from close to where you park your car - just look for gaps in the trees and between the buildings; hundreds of gulls roost on these ponds and the little islands also support herons, stilts and a few duck.

6. Falesia lagoon is found by continuing on the main road into Vilamoura and turning right (37.0898N, 8.1237W) on the Avda da Praia de Falesia (Falesia Beach). Follow this road around to the left after 300 metres and turn right at the next junction; Falesia lagoon then appears on your right after 250 metres. Park by the bridge (37.0842N, 8.1274W) and scan around, also checking the reedbed on the other side of the road. The waterbirds are usually just common stuff such as Mallard, Little Grebe and Cormorant but Marsh Harrier and Purple Heron often fly over or drop in. Black-shouldered Kite has often been seen on the telegraph wires beyond the lagoon, especially in the winter months. Others have had Little Bittern, Purple Gallinule, Black Tern and Great Reed Warbler here.

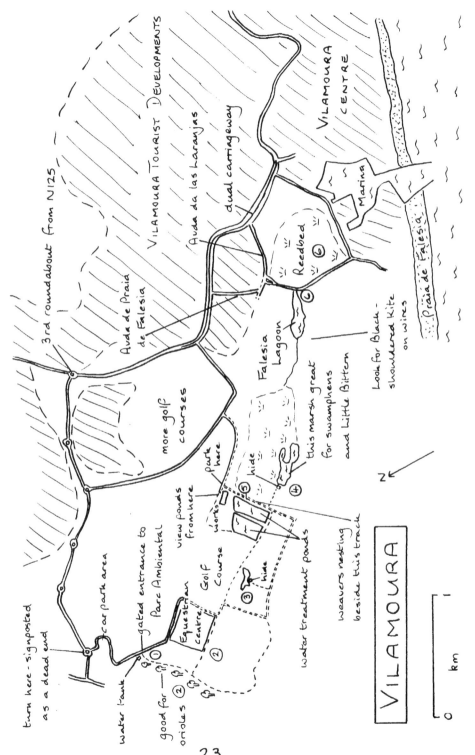

VILAMOURA

turn here - signposted as a dead end

water tank

good for orioles ②

gated entrance to Parc Ambiental

car park area

Equestrian centre ②

view ponds from here

Golf Course

water works

park here

③ hide

water treatment ponds

weavers nesting beside this track

⑤ hide

④

this marsh great for swamphens and Little Bittern

more golf courses

3rd roundabout from N125

Avda de Praia de Falesia

VILAMOURA TOURIST DEVELOPMENTS

Avda de las Laranjas

dual carriageway

Falesia Lagoon

Reedbed ⑥

⑦

Look for Black-shouldered Kite on wires

VILAMOURA CENTRE

Marina

Praia de Falesia

N

km

0   1

23

Ria Formosa West – Quinta do Lago and Ludo

Attraction

The Ria Formosa is a tidal lagoon, almost 60 km long, almost cut off from the sea by a string of sandy barrier islands. It supports internationally important numbers of wintering and passage waders and birds such as Caspian Tern, Audouin's Gull, Spoonbill and wintering Bluethroat can be seen almost anywhere along its length. The most popular spot for birders though is between Quinta do Lago and the airport as this area also has two small but very attractive pools where birds such as Purple Swamphen can be seen at close range.

Getting there

The easiest access is via the last roundabout before Faro airport. From there follow signs to Praia do Faro then, after 500 metres, take a right turn (37.0222N, 7.9761W) marked by a sign to a restaurant. After 800 metres, keep left at the roundabout (sign to 'Pontal') and follow this track as far as you can, stopping at sites en route. Although there is a large gateway with signs saying 'Acesso Prohibido', visitors usually drive beyond here almost as far as the golf course.

Notes

1. The track passes a pine plantation which supports large numbers of Azure-winged Magpies. Watch for flocks of them darting through the trees.

2. The next clearing on the left is worth checking as it is a regular hunting area for Black-shouldered Kite, which often perches on the telegraph poles or wires.

3. Keep driving until a lush, reed-fringed lake appears on the right-hand side (37.0317N, 7.9946W). This is Ludo pool or the Foz de Ribeira de São Lourenço. It's only small but it can be packed with a selection of ducks, coots and grebes including dozens of Wigeon, Gadwall and Pintail. Herons such as Night Heron, Purple Heron and Little Bittern are all possible and it's worth checking the Coots because Red-knobbed Coot has been found on several occasions. Regular raptors here include not just Buzzard and Marsh Harrier but also Osprey and Booted Eagle which winters here. I've had Goshawk and Black-shouldered Kite from this spot too. You'll surely hear Cetti's Warbler and possibly Penduline Tit in winter.

4. Opposite the lake is a tidal creek and saltpans where you might see birds such as flamingoes, stilts, avocets and possibly Caspian Terns.

5. Park at the end of the saltpans (37.0279N, 8.0047W) and follow the track between the golf-course and another arm of the tidal creek. This track leads along an avenue of eucalyptus trees towards a bungalow via a raised hill which gives views over the creek. In winter, this is likely to have hundreds of Wigeon and dozens of flamingoes, Spoonbills, Cormorants and waders including Avocets and you might also see Dartford Warbler and Stone Curlew around the hill. The next site is reached via a parallel path, closer to the golf course (marked by posts with blue triangles), past the Roman ruins.

6. Despite being little more than an ornamental pond surrounded by a golf course, the Lagoa do São Laurenço, commonly referred to as Quinta do Lago lake, is a beautiful spot for birdwatching, not least because there is an excellent tower hide (37.0246N, 8.0118W) at the edge of the footpath. From this hide you are pretty much guaranteed lots of close views of Purple Swamphen and there's also a good chance of birds such as Little Bittern, Glossy Ibis, Red-crested Pochard and Black-headed Weaver (which breeds here). The lake holds a variety of diving ducks, dabbling ducks, grebes and herons including regular Squacco Heron. It's a good place to stare into the reeds for reedbed warblers, waxbills and Little Crakes and rarer species seen here have included Great Bittern, White-headed Duck and Marbled Duck. A visit at dusk in spring or summer should produce Red-necked Nightjar. The pinewoods intermingled with the golf course are good for Hoopoe, Azure-winged Magpie, Iberian Green Wopodpecker, Firecrest and Short-toed Treecreeper. I've had Siskins in February, Golden Oriole in April and Subalpine Warbler in October and William Oliver has also had Hawfinch and Crossbill, plus Orphean and Olivaceous and Warblers.

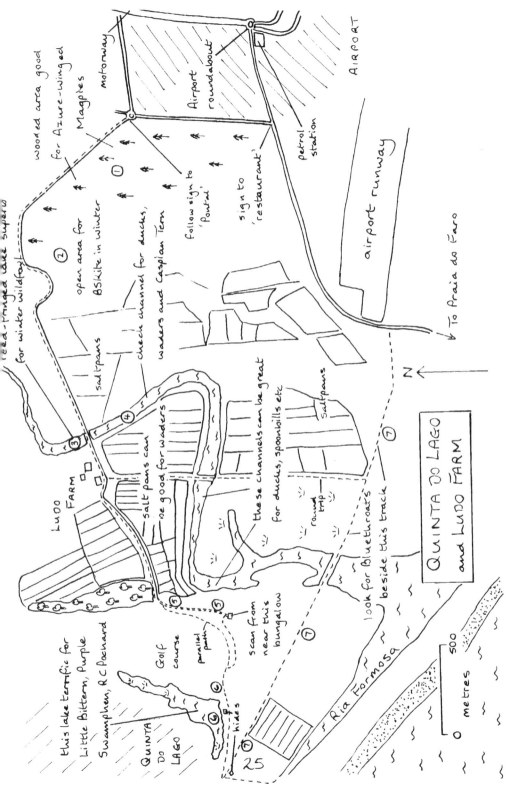

QUINTA DO LAGO and LUDO FARM

motorway

Airport roundabout

AIRPORT

petrol station

sign to 'restaurant'

Follow sign to 'Pontal'

airport runway

Wooded area good for Azure-winged Magpies

reed-fringed lake superb for winter wildfowl

open area for BS/kite in winter

check channel for ducks, waders and Caspian Tern

salt-pans

① ② ③ ④ ⑤ ⑥ ⑦

LUDO FARM

salt pans can be good for waders

these channels can be great for ducks, spoonbills etc

round trip

Salt-pans

look for Bluethroats beside this track

N

To Praia do Faro

this lake terrific for Little Bittern, Purple Swamphen, R.C. Pochard

Golf course

parallel path

scan from near this bungalow

QUINTA DO LAGO

hides

Ria Formosa

metres
0   500

25

7. The path beyond the hide brings you out to the estuary, overlooked by another hide (37.0246N, 8.0155W) though birds from here are usually quite distant and against the light. By turning left in front of this hide you can walk along a track past the saltpans either back to the Praia do Faro road or back to Ludo farm to make a round trip. From these paths you should see the usual estuarine waders and ducks plus flamingoes, spoonbills, Caspian Terns and Bluethroats.

8. Alternatively, from this estuary hide you can follow a nature trail west along the edge of the Ria Formosa, past a brackish pool on the right to an old, rather small set of saltpans (Red-necked Phalarope twice here in spring) and, beyond those to larger saltpans where the usual waders, Mediterranean Gulls, Caspian Terns, Spoonbills and Bluethroats are likely.

9. Even further west is another pool, the Lagoa de Dunas Douradas which can be good for waterbirds. To get there, follow signs from Quinta do Lago towards Vale de Lobo but turn south to Garrao. Follow the main street through Garrao until you see a left turn to Garrao poente. This takes you past the lagoon on the left. Park opposite the Dunas Douradas Beach Club (37.0439N, 8.0550W) and walk back along a trail on the west side of the pool. An observation tower (37.0446N, 8.0528W) gives better views. In addition to the usual Little Grebes, Coots and Cormorants, there are breeding Black-headed Weavers and Little Bitterns are also found in spring. If water levels are high, look for waders in the pools you can see from the boardwalk to the beach.

10. The airport waterworks or ETAR pools (37.0165N, 7.9570W) were briefly excellent in the 1990's when birds such as White-headed Duck, White-winged Black Tern, Grey Phalarope and Black-necked Grebes were found. However, they have been usurped by a modern waterworks complex which is no longer attractive to birds and the nearest saltpans were completely dry and devoid of birds when I visited in October 2012.

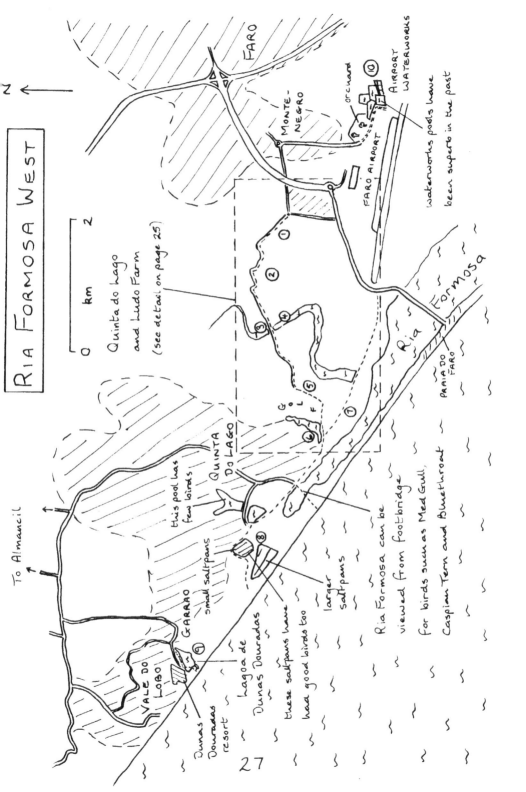

RIA FORMOSA WEST

N ←

0   km   2

Quinta do Lago
and Ludo Farm
(see detail on page 25)

FARO

MONTE-
NEGRO

orchard

⑩

AIRPORT
WATERWORKS

FARO AIRPORT

Waterworks pools have
been superb in the past

Ria Formosa

PRAIA DO
FARO

Ria Formosa can be
viewed from footbridge

For birds such as Med Gull,
Caspian Tern and Bluethroat

larger
saltpans

⑧

these saltpans have
had good birds too

Lagoa de
Dunas Douradas

small saltpans

GARRÃO

this pool has
few birds

QUINTA
DO LAGO

⑨

Dunas
Douradas
resort

VALE DO
LOBO

To Almancil

① ② ③ ④ ⑤ ⑥ ⑦

27

Ria Formosa east – Olhao to Tavira

Attraction

This part of the Ria Formosa gets less attention than the area around Faro but is equally good for estuarine and saltpan birds, such as flamingoes, spoonbills, avocets and wintering Bluethroats. This is a better area for gulls including lots of Mediterranean Gulls, breeding Audouin's Gulls and regular Slender-billed Gulls.

Getting there

From the N22, take roads signposted to either Olhao or Tavira and access these sites from the N125 road which runs between those two towns.

Notes

1. One of the best ways to experience the Ria Formosa is to take a boat trip through the estuarine channels. For example, formosamar.com run a cruise from Olhao to Fuseta which is great for birdwatchers. Try to book when the tide is at its lowest. The boat will take you close to lots of estuarine waders and you are also likely to see Spoonbills, Mediterranean Gulls and Audouin's Gulls (which breed on one of the barrier islands off Olhao).

2. The Quinta de Marim is the location of the headquarters of the Ria Formosa national park, set in modest grounds which include a nature trail and visitor centre. The walk takes you through habitat for birds such as Dartford, Cetti's and Fan-tailed Warblers to hides overlooking two lagoons. One of these is a freshwater pool where you may see only a few grebes, coots and dabbling duck but Purple Swamphens are here too and Little Bittern is sometimes seen. The other pool is tidal and, if water levels are right, can provide a feast of waders to scan through; in April we had lots of Bar-tailed Godwit, Knot, Grey Plover and stilts amongst hundreds of Dunlin and a smattering of other species. To get to the reserve from the A-22, take the N125 towards Olhao, until, 300 metres after the roundabout, you see a road to the left signposted to Ria Formosa reserve. Follow this road for 900 metres to the gates (37.0329N, 7.8221W) of the reserve on the left. There's a small entrance fee (2.60 Euros each in 2013) which entitles you to drive a little closer into the reserve. The barrier closes at 8pm in summer.

3. Many of the seabirds you can see off Sagres can also be viewed, often in calmer waters and from a bigger boat, by taking a pelagic trip with formosamar.com from Fuseta out into the open waters beyond the barrier islands. Here you are soon at the edge of the continental shelf and the local fishing boats attract flocks of gulls and other seabirds. By chumming in their vicinity you should get great views of petrels, shearwaters and skuas at least from July to September. When you return to Fuseta, the lunch of fresh barbequed fish at Casa Corvo on the quayside is an experience not to be missed (unless you are vegetarian).

4. The coastal side of the town of Tavira has saltpans which extend for some kilometres in both directions. Here you can watch lots of waders and gulls, including Audouin's and regular Slender-billed. The 4-star Hotel Albacora is located close to great birding habitat. A walk from here (37.1198N, 7.6256W) towards the Rio Gilao should produce a variety of waders (including impressive numbers of Stone Curlew) plus Spoonbill, Bluethroat (in winter) and gulls (someone in our party counted 15 Slender-billed). To get there, follow signs to 'Zona commercial' at the eastern end of Tavira then, when you get to this shopping centre, follow signs to Forte do Rato. Check the saltpans and creeks en route but continue past the fort, park near the hotel and explore the area between here and the river. Another good spot is at 'Quatro Aguas' on the other side of the Rio Gilao. To get there from Tavira, follow signs to the beach and look for a track (37.1176N, 7.6310W) into the saltpans to the right just before you reach the quay. This is a particularly good spot for watching gulls, especially Audouin's.

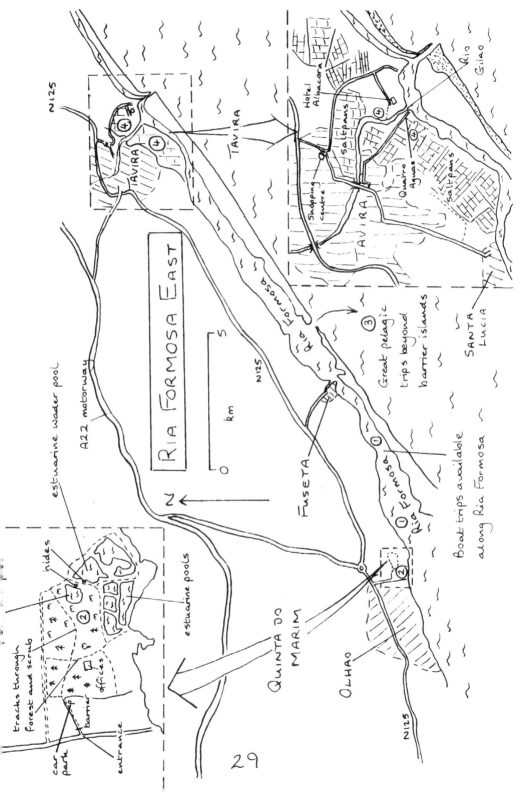

Ria Formosa East

N125

TAVIRA

Hotel Albacora

Saltpans

Rio Gilão

Shopping centre

Quatro Aguas

Saltpans

TAVIRA

TAVIRA

SANTA LUCIA

A22 motorway

estuarine wader pool

N

km

0   5

N125

Rio Formosa

③ Great pelagic trips beyond barrier islands

①

Rio Formosa

① Ria Formosa

FUSETA

Boat trips available along Ria Formosa

②

QUINTA DO MARIM

OLHÃO

N125

hides

tracks through forest and scrub

②

estuarine pools

offices

car park

barrier

entrance

29

Castro Marim

Attraction

On the Portuguese side of the Ria Guadiana are 2 sets of saltpans which can be good for ducks, waders, flamingoes and gulls, including Slender-billed and breeding Audouin's, and a flood-plain with special breeding birds such as Little Bustard, Lesser Short-toed Lark and Spectacled Warbler. However, despite (or because of) this being a nature reserve, access is very limited and most birds have to be viewed at a distance.

Getting there

The last junction before Spain on the IP1 motorway is signposted south to Castro Marim and Vila Real de Santo Antonio. The best habitats can be easily reached from there.

Notes

1. The best access to the saltpans east of Castro Marim is from the north. As you drive north from Castro Marim, look for a track to the right (37.2346N, 7.4474W) signposted to 'reserva natural' and follow this as far as a car park and a monstrous (and usually closed) reserve headquarters (37.2309N, 7.4264W). En route, you will pass the first of the saltpan lagoons in which you may get your best views of shanks, godwits and sandpipers. From the visitor centre you can scan northwards over pools that often have ducks such as Red-crested Pochard and maybe herons such as Spoonbills. However, for the best birding, walk south from the car park and encircle the raised hill. It is no longer possible to walk into the saltpans from here so you have to hope that birds such as Lesser Short-toed Lark and Spectacled Warbler are singing close enough to the hill to be located; this is difficult outside the breeding season. In April 2013, the bushes on the slope of the hill (37.2285N, 7.4250W) had a Great Spotted Cuckoo and a singing Spectacled Warbler and Lesser Short-toed Lark was just about audible nearby. The hill provides a good vantage point from which, with a scope, you can scan the saltpans for gulls, terns, herons and waders (Spoonbills, Marsh Harriers and Caspian Terns are regular) and also the floodplain close to the river for Little Bustard. These are easiest to spot in spring when they are displaying but you may be lucky to see small parties in winter too.

2. Between Castro Marim and Vila Real, the road crosses a creek which makes an interesting lagoon. Park by this bridge and check to the west of the road for ducks, waders and herons. Black-necked Grebes are regular here in winter and it's a good spot to look for hunting Montagu's Harriers in summer.

3. The saltpans to the west of Castro Marim are best reached via the N125-6. Immediately south of a bridge (Pont de Este Veira) is a track (37.2135N, 7.4708W) leading east to the entrance to the saltworks. There is no public access beyond their gate (so you can no longer walk south past the productive freshwater marsh just beyond the farm) but there's a track leading west from here (37.2094N, 7.4636W) which continues for 4 km around the north of the saltpans. This allows you to get closer to birds that can be seen distantly from the gate such as hundreds of flamingoes, Spoonbills, Avocets, Cormorants, waders and gulls including breeding Audouin's Gulls and regular Slender-billed Gulls. Pratincoles can often be seen here too. The same track can be reached from the east side: as you drive south from Castro Marim, look for a cut down palm tree topped by a stork's nest then take the next sandy track (37.2054N, 7.4336W) to the right towards the first of 2 ruined farm buildings. Park near the ruin (37.2047N, 7.4355W) and walk from there.

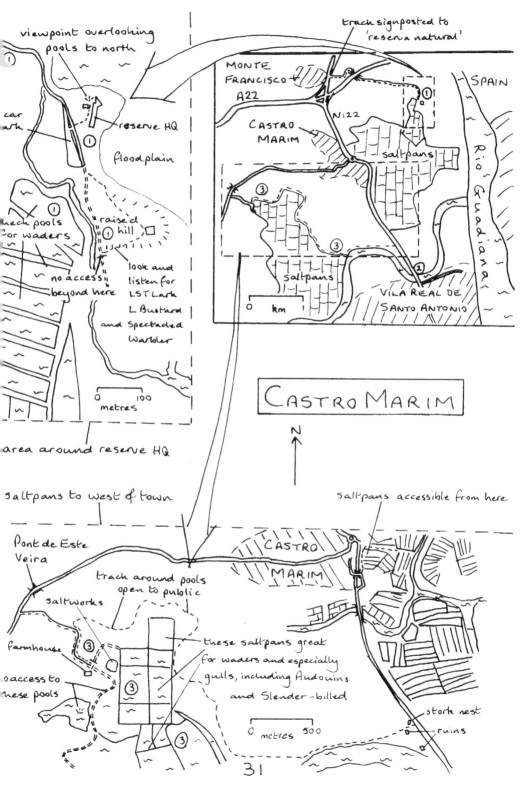

Castro Verde

Attraction

This is by far the best area of grassland steppe in Portugal; much grander and wilder than the plains around Elvas or Evora. However, the greater scale of suitable habitat could mean that the birds are harder to find here, especially in winter when the bustards are concentrated into flocks. In spring though, it is a fabulous area, full of displaying bustards, singing larks, calling sandgrouse and hunting Rollers and raptors, which nowadays may include Spanish Imperial Eagle, Bonelli's Eagle and Black Vulture.

Getting there

Castro Verde is about 100 km north of the Algarve and therefore easily reachable in a day via the A2 to Castro Verde (toll road), the E1/N264 to Ourique (no toll) or the N122 to Mertola.

Notes

1. Black-shouldered Kites are quite numerous in the winter months and should easily be seen during any drive around the area as long as you also stop and scan from good vantage points. In spring however they can be more elusive and may be easier to find outside of the main plains area. For example, the area between Ourique and Castro Verde looks particularly promising; remember to look especially where the trees are more spaced out. One site where they have been found in spring is along the 'acesso local' track (37.6619N, 8.1769W) which leads south from the main road, opposite the signposted turn-off to Aldea de Grandaços. Other birds here include Woodlark, Azure-winged Magpie and Woodchat Shrike.

2. Many of the best areas for bustards are managed by the Ligue por Protecion de Nature (LPN) but are out of bounds to birdwatchers. The LPN also ask you not to drive down farm tracks as this may upset the farmers. They do however offer guided walks to show visitors the best birds and they will point out for you the best places where birds have been showing well during the week before. To take advantage of these services, visit their information centre near Entradas. To get there from Castro Verde, take the IP2 towards Beja and look for a turning to the right (37.7328N, 8.0569W) just before km 384 to get onto a parallel slip road. Follow this for 1.9 km then turn right, signposted to Centro de Educaçao Ambiental. The centre (37.7364N, 8.0314W), which is 1.5 km down this track, is worth visiting in its own right as there is a water tower with breeding Lesser Kestrels, Little Bustards call in the surrounding fields and Rollers breed in the nearby buildings. The centre also offers the chance of using photographic hides to get you really close to birds such as Roller, Lesser Kestrel, Little Owl and bustards but you need to book these well in advance. The following sites are all either on public roads or on tracks recommended by LPN.

3. The road to the north-west from Entradas (signposted to Carregueiro) makes a good vantage point for looking for bustards (and Black-shouldered Kite in winter) and it was from here that I photographed close-up Montagu's Harriers and Roller in April 2013. There's a colony of White Storks in a eucalyptus tree (37.7940N, 8.0555W) which, as is usual here, has Spanish Sparrows breeding in the stork nests; there are also Red-rumped Swallows nesting under the nearby bridge.

4. The road leading south-east from Entradas to São Marcos do Ataboeira isn't shown on some maps. To find it, turn into Entradas village opposite the road to Carregueiro, then turn right then quickly left in the village so you pass the restaurant (37.7708N, 8.0155W) on your left. Follow this road all the way to São Marcos. Before racing to site 5, it may be worth checking the fields closest to the village since in autumn, flocks of Great Bustards come to feed on fallen olives around the olive groves close to town. Navigate your way to the cemetery (37.7722N, 8.0076W) on the edge of the village and explore from there.

5. In spring, one of the best areas for all the steppe species is on the Entradas to São Marcos road, just south of the Monte Novo trig point. Park by the road between here and the next farm building (eg 37.7452N, 7.9961W) and scan the fields to the south-west. The nearest field has Little Bustards which can be seen displaying close to the road. The area beyond there is good for Black-bellied Sandgrouse; in April 2013 we made several visits and never failed to see up to 20 sandgrouse plus other birds such as Lesser Kestrel, Great Bustard, Stone Curlew, Montagu's Harrier, Tawny Pipit, Short-toed Lark and Calandra Lark.

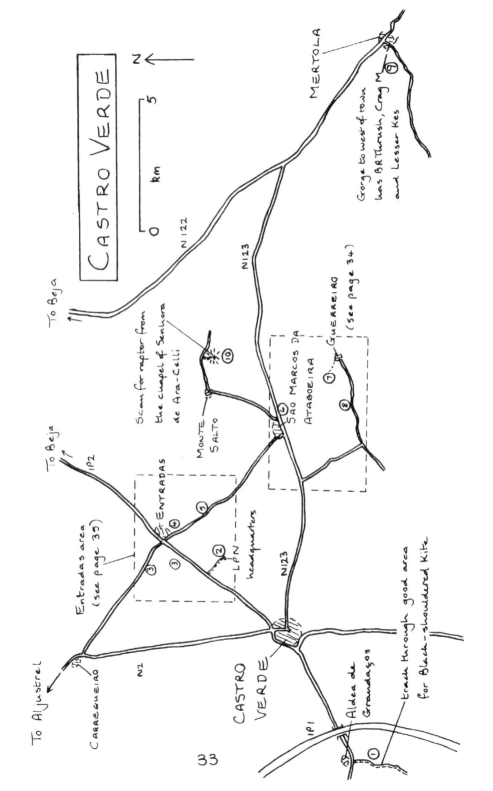

CASTRO VERDE

N ←

0   km   5

N 122

To Beja

To Beja
IP2

Entradas area
(see page 35)

Entradas

④
⑤
③
③
② LPN
    headquarters

CARREGUEIRO

N2

To Aljustrel

CASTRO
VERDE

IP1

Aldea de
Grandaços

①

track through good area
for Black-shouldered Kite

N123

Scan for raptor from
the chapel of Senhora
de Ara-Celli

⑩

MONTE
SALTO

⑥ SÃO MARCOS DA
  ATABOEIRA

⑦ GUERREIRO
  (see page 34)

⑧

N123

N122

MERTOLA

⑨

Gorge to west of town
has BRThrush, Crag M
and Lesser Kes

33

6. The most popular place for seeing bustards is the LPN reserve on the plains south of São Marcos da Ataboeira. As the N123 passes the town, look for gates on the opposite side of the road labelled LPN, from which you can often see bustards. 1.6 km east of the village you can get off the main road and scan from a slip road (37.7080N, 9.9194W) behind some eucalyptus trees. From there we had great views of bustards in flight and also 2 juvenile Spanish Imperial Eagles with a flock of Black and Griffon Vultures.

7. However, in my opinion, a much better bet is to approach this reserve from the south via the village of Guerriero. As you enter the village, keep left until you reach a track which climbs up the far hillside. At least in spring you should see both species of bustard from this track. Park 1400 metres from the village (eg 37.6770N, 7.8990W) and look on the slope to the north for displaying Great Bustards (I had at least 20 in 2009) and to the south for Little Bustards. Continue to the plateau where a gate signifies the entrance to the bustard reserve. The area close to this gate is especially good for Little Bustards and Calandra Larks and you're likely to see Great Bustards further away.

8. Nearby, in 2008 I had several views of Black-bellied Sandgrouse (parties of 2, 2 and 7) flying over the road between Viseus and Alcaria del Coelho and settling in the fields to the north of the km 16.5 marker. There were several Montagu's Harrier along this road and 4 Stone Curlews too.

9. The picturesque hill-top town of Mertola has a castle and a convent in and around which both species of kestrel breed. A good birdwatching spot is the bridge over the river Oeiras. To get there, drive through the town following signs to Vila Real de Santo Antonio; you'll see the gorge as you leave the town. With patience you should see Crag Martin and Blue Rock Thrush here and sometimes Rock Bunting too. Even better, at least in spring, are the pairs of Lesser Kestrels which nest in boxes on the supports of the bridge and can be seen flying below you if you stand near the bridge (37.6381N, 7.6669W).

10. In recent years, the Castro Verde plains have become increasingly visited by the bigger raptors such as vultures and eagles. Soaring groups of Griffon Vultures often carry a few Black Vultures with them; Golden and Spanish Imperial Eagles are now seen regularly and Bonelli's Eagles breed here, unusually, in trees not on cliffs. There's a chance of these raptors almost anywhere east of Castro Verde but a good place to scan for them is from the chapel of Nossa Senhora de Ara-Celli. To get there, take the N123 east from São Marcos de Ataboeira but turn almost immediately left on the road signposted to Salto. Follow this road, past Salto for a further 2.2 km then look for a turn to the right (37.7514N, 7.8888N), opposite a set of extravagant gates. This road climbs to the chapel where you can park and scan. I had two Imperial Eagles en route to the chapel and views of Booted and Short-toed Eagle from the verandah.

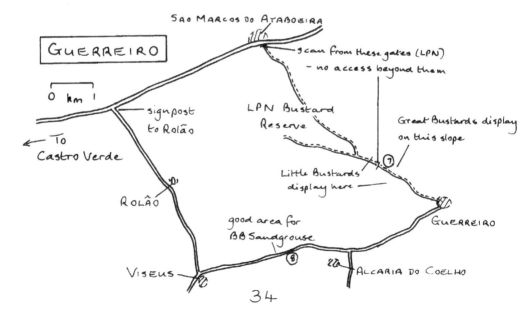

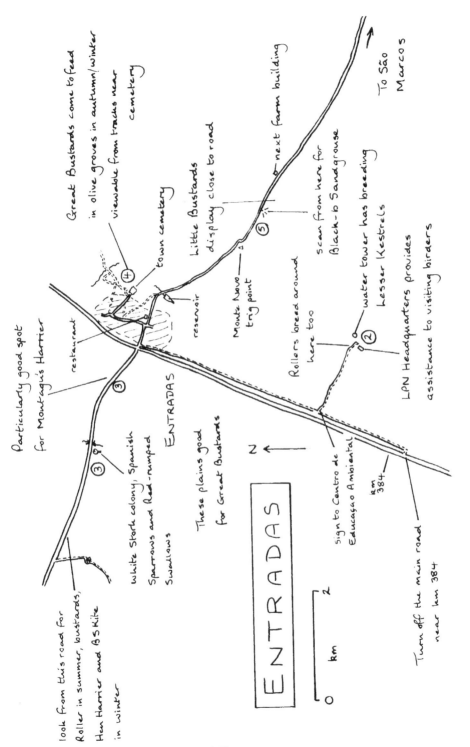

Particularly good spot
for Montagu's Harrier

Great Bustards come to feed
in olive groves in autumn/winter
viewable from tracks near
cemetery

town cemetery

restaurant

Little Bustards
display close to road

reservoir

Monte Novo
trig point

next farm building

To São
Marcos

Rollers breed around
here too

scan from here for
Black-b Sandgrouse

water tower has breeding
Lesser Kestrels

LPN Headquarters provides
assistance to visiting birders

White Stork colony, Spanish
Sparrows and Red-rumped
Swallows

These plains good
for Great Bustards

N ←

ENTRADAS

sign to Centro de
Educação Ambiental

km
384

Turn off the main road
near km 384

look from this road for
Rollers in summer, bustards,
Hen Harrier and B5 Kite
in winter

ENTRADAS

km
0   2

35

Elvas

Attraction

This really small site offers excellent chances to see steppe birds such as Little and Great Bustard, Stone Curlew and Montagu's Harrier but it is Black-shouldered Kite that makes this site so special. Whilst this is an easy species to see in southern Portugal or Extremadura in winter, in summer it can be much more elusive; in 2013 I spent nearly a month in those areas without seeing that species but here I found 6 Black-shouldered Kites in less than an hour.

Getting there

From the Spanish side, drive into Portugal on the A6, then take the turning to 'Elvas este'. After 1.5 km, take the turning left (38.8875N, 7.1286W) opposite the red-roofed factories to take one of the roads in the triangle shown on the map. Alternatively, from Elvas, follow signs to Forte de Santa Luzia until, at the roundabout next to a Lidl store, you take a right turn (38.8747N, 7.1586W) signposted to the Forte. Follow this road past the Forte to the plains beyond.

Notes

1. Coming from the Forte de Santa Luzia, once you pass the highest part of the road you begin to get views over large areas of countryside. Stop and scan wherever you get an open view as there's a chance of both Great and Little Bustard, especially in winter when up to 220 Little Bustards have been seen. This stretch of road also sometimes has Black-shouldered Kite and (Iberian) Great Grey Shrike.

2. The best area is where the fields on the left include a scattering of oak trees (eg 38.8523N, 7.1188W). The trees themselves make nesting sites for Black-shouldered Kite and Black Kite, both of which are easy to see in spring and summer when Montagu's Harrier and Stone Curlew are also present. The fields on the opposite side of the road seemed to have breeding Montagu's Harriers and in winter there are often Great Bustards there.

3. After passing the reservoir on the left you'll see a large low-lying field on the right (38.8433N, 7.1045W). This is a particularly popular site for Little Bustards in winter.

4. Beyond the T-junction at the bottom of the road, the fields have areas that are wet enough to support Marsh Harriers, Great Reed Warblers and, sometimes, Collared Pratincoles.

5. There are further opportunities to scan for Great Bustards on the road back to Elvas along the right-hand side of the triangle.

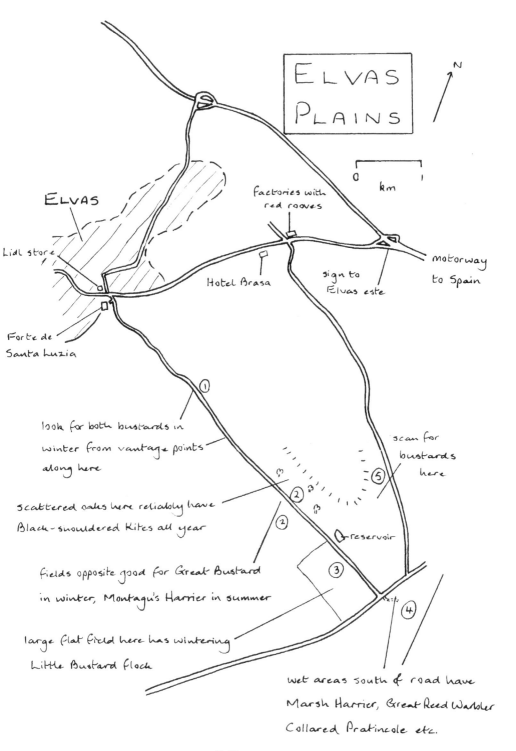

ELVAS PLAINS

N

ELVAS

Lidl store

Factories with red rooves

Hotel Brasa

sign to Elvas este

motorway to Spain

0 — km — 1

Forte de Santa Luzia

① look for both bustards in winter from vantage points along here

scan for bustards here

⑤

scattered oaks here reliably have Black-shouldered Kites all year

② ③

②

⑤ reservoir

fields opposite good for Great Bustard in winter, Montagu's Harrier in summer

③

large flat field here has wintering Little Bustard flock

④

wet areas south of road have Marsh Harrier, Great Reed Warbler Collared Pratincole etc.

Algarve Hills

Attraction

The range of hills just inland from the Algarve coast includes several areas that can be good for birds such as Rock Bunting, White-rumped Swift, Black-eared Wheatear, Rufous Bush-chat, Iberian Chiffchaff and a variety of eagles. They also happen to be scenically very attractive. The notes below describe my experiences at a number of sites that were recommended in the book 'Birdwatching Guide to the Algarve' by João Ministro (referred to here as 'the Algarve Guide').

Getting there

Monchique is inland from Portimao, Barranco do Velho is north of Faro and Alcoutim is off the road between Castro Marim and Mertola (see map on inside cover).

Notes

1. Mount Foia is the highest point in the Algarve. Many birders visit this site in search of species such as Rock Bunting, Dartford Warbler and Blue Rock Thrush but the Algarve guide particularly recommends it as a site for eagles. Apparently Bonelli's are seen regularly and Golden Eagle occasionally but I found only Short-toed Eagle. Rock Bunting was easily seen in the open areas beyond the car park (eg 37.3167N, 8.5920W). I also had at least 3 pairs of Blue Rock Thrush but Dartford Warbler was elusive. Instead I found a Whitethroat and a singing Melodious Warbler. Alpine Accentor has been seen regularly in winter but beware, it can be very cold up there even in May. To get there, take the scenic N266 north from Portimao then, when you reach Monchique, follow signs to Mount Foia.

2. The Algarve Guide recommends the slopes below Picota as the best for woodland birds. I took the turning from Monchique towards Alferce, then turned right after 500 metres on a very minor road towards Picota. After just 1 km, the woods on both sides of the road (37.3158N, 8.5436W) had Iberian Green Woodpecker, Iberian Chiffchaff, Hawfinch and Firecrest.

3. According to the Algarve guide, Bonelli's Eagles are easy to see around Barranco do Velho. As you leave the north end of town, there is a church on the left. Look for a track (starting at 37.2412N, 7.9398W) which passes behind this church as you get terrific views to the west from here. I didn't actually see any eagles but did hear Golden Oriole in the valley below.

4. A better place for orioles is along the lush valley at Fonte de Benemola, where I also had lots of song-birds such as Nightingale, Cetti's Warbler, Iberian Chiffchaff and Melodious Warbler and all 3 species of woodpecker. To get there from Barranco, follow signs to Loulé, then Querenca until you pick up signs for Fonte de Benemola, a local tourist attraction. As you approach the valley, turn off into the car park on the right (37.1985N, 8.0046W) and walk from there.

5. Another way to look for raptors is to take the very minor road (M513) to the east from Barranco do Velho towards Cabeza do Velho. There's a chance of raptors all along here, especially from the viewpoint just before Cabeza do Velho (37.2437N, 7.8340W) but the only eagles on my visit were Short-toed. The Algarve Guide recommends a walk in the cultivated areas just north of Parizes and here we had Golden Oriole, Dartford Warbler, Subalpine Warbler and several Melodious Warblers. Further west is a junction (37.2410N, 7.9115W) with a track leading south to Menta. A walk for 2 km along the road west from the river yielded Rock Bunting, Iberian Chiffchaff, Iberian Green Woodpecker, Melodious Warbler, Dartford Warbler and Crag Martin.

6. Between Odeleite and Foz de Odeleite is a river valley which makes an attractive walk. Here I had good views of Golden Oriole and glimpses of Dartford Warbler and Rock Bunting but the best birds were two Bonelli's Eagles which glided low over the valley. To get there from Odeleite, follow signs to Foz de Odeleite and, after 1 km, look for the track to the left into the valley below. Park and walk from there (37.3389N, 7.4835W).

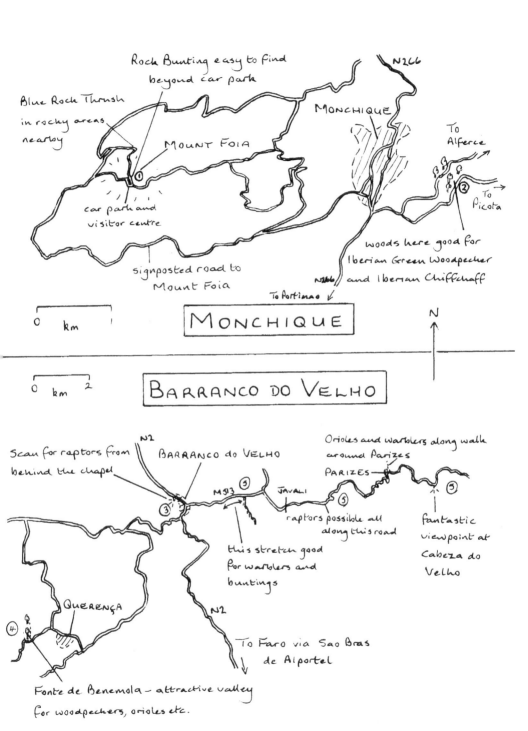

Rock Bunting easy to find
beyond car park

Blue Rock Thrush
in rocky areas
nearby

MOUNT FOIA

N266

MONCHIQUE

To
Alferce

To
Picota

car park and
visitor centre

woods here good for
Iberian Green Woodpecker
and Iberian Chiffchaff

N266

signposted road to
Mount Foia

To Portimao ↓

0   km   1

MONCHIQUE

N
↑

0   km   2

BARRANCO DO VELHO

N2

Scan for raptors from
behind the chapel

BARRANCO do VELHO

Orioles and warblers along walk
around Parizes

PARIZES

M513

JAVALI

raptors possible all
along this road

fantastic
viewpoint at
Cabeza do
Velho

this stretch good
for warblers and
buntings

QUERENÇA

N2

To Faro via Sao Bras
de Alportel

Fonte de Benemola – attractive valley
for woodpeckers, orioles etc.

39

7. The Algarve Guide suggests that the Alcoutim area offers the best chance of finding Olivaceous Warbler, Rufous Bush Chat and White-rumped Swift. The first 2 species are often associated with river valleys so, having failed to find them at site 6, I checked all the sites where streams flowed under the road from Foz de Odeleite to Alcoutim. In late April, maybe I was too early for the Bush Chat (and almost certainly the swift) but I failed to hear any Olivaceous Warblers. I did however see a Little Bittern under the bridge next to the roman villa at Laranjeiras (37.4037N, 7.4599W). Some of these bridges had Red-rumped Swallows which in turn might attract White-rumped Swifts to take over their nests. Alcoutim itself had Golden Orioles by the river and the road to the north of Alcoutim, towards Mertola, had Rock Buntings, Black-eared Wheatears and Iberian Grey Shrikes.

8. The Algarve Guide also recommended the reservoir at Pereiro, stressing that an early morning visit is best. I therefore assumed it must be a great site for songbirds, perhaps surrounded by waterside bushes for Olivaceous Warbler. But no, it was a very open, quite barren site where the best birds were Short-toed Larks, Little Ringed Plovers and a few Collared Pratincoles. The village is signposted from the IC27 opposite the turning to Alcoutim and the reservoir is on the left of this road just before the village (turn into the car park at 37.4458N, 7.5893W).

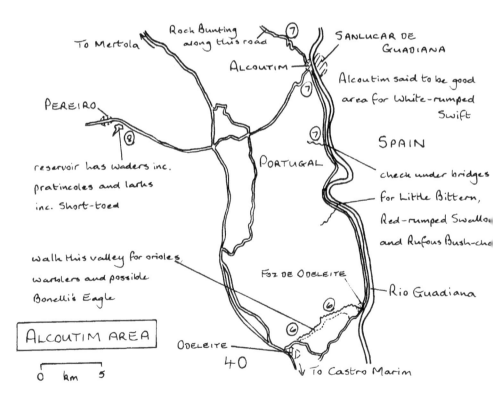

To Mertola
Rock Bunting along this road
SANLUCAR DE GUADIANA
ALCOUTIM
Alcoutim said to be good area for White-rumped Swift
PEREIRO
SPAIN
reservoir has waders inc. pratincoles and larks inc. Short-toed
PORTUGAL
check under bridges for Little Bittern, Red-rumped Swallow and Rufous Bush-chat
walk this valley for orioles warblers and possible Bonelli's Eagle
FOZ DE ODELEITE
Rio Guadiana
ALCOUTIM AREA
ODELEITE
40
To Castro Marim
0   km   5